YOUTH WITH CULTURAL/
LANGUAGE DIFFERENCES

Interpreting an
Alien World

HELPING YOUTH WITH MENTAL, PHYSICAL, AND SOCIAL CHALLENGES

Title List

YOUTH WITH CULTURAL/
LANGUAGE DIFFERENCES

Interpreting an Alien World

by Kenneth McIntosh
and Ida Walker

Mason Crest Publishers
Philadelphia

Mason Crest Publishers Inc.
370 Reed Road
Broomall, Pennsylvania 19008
(866) MCP-BOOK (toll free)
www.masoncrest.com

First printing

1 2 3 4 5 6 7 8 9 10

ISBN 978-1-4222-0133-6 (series)

Library of Congress Cataloging-in-Publication Data

McIntosh, Kenneth, 1959–

  Youth with cultural/language differences : interpreting an alien world / by Kenneth McIntosh and Ida Walker.

     p. cm. — (Helping youth with mental, physical, and social challenges)

  Includes bibliographical references and index.

  ISBN-13: 978-1-4222-0141-1

  1. Youth with social disabilities—Juvenile literature. 2. Minority youth—Juvenile literature. 3. Children of immigrants—Juvenile literature. 4. Gang members—Juvenile literature. 5. Prejudices—Juvenile literature. I. Walker, Ida. II. Title.

HV1421.M42 2008

362.7089—dc22

2006031786

Interior pages produced by
Harding House Publishing Service, Inc.
www.hardinghousepages.com
Interior design by MK Bassett-Harvey.
Cover design by MK Bassett-Harvey.
Cover Illustration by Keith Rosko.
Printed in the Hashemite Kingdom of Jordan.

Contents

Introduction

We are all people first, before anything else. Our shared humanity is more important than the impressions we give to each other by how we look, how we learn, or how we act. Each of us is worthy simply because we are all part of the human race. Though we are all different in many ways, we can celebrate our differences as well as our similarities.

In this book series, you will read about many young people with various special needs that impact their lives in different ways. The disabilities are not *who* the people are, but the disabilities are an important characteristic of each person. When we recognize that we all have differing needs, we can grow toward greater awareness and tolerance of each other. Just as important, we can learn to accept our differences.

Not all young people with a disability are the same as the persons in the stories. But you will learn from these stories how a special need impacts a young person, as well as his or her family and friends. The story will help you understand differences better and appreciate how differences make us all stronger and better.

—*Cindy Croft, M.A.Ed.*

Did you know that as many as 8 percent of teens experience anxiety or depression, and as many as 70 to 90 percent will use substances such as alcohol or illicit drugs at some time? Other young people are living with life-threatening diseases including HIV infection and cancer, as well as chronic psychiatric conditions such as bipolar disease and schizophrenia. Still other teens have the challenge of being "different" from peers because they are intellectually gifted, are from another culture, or have trouble controlling their behavior or socializing with others. All youth with challenges experience additional stresses compared to their typical peers. The good news is that there are many resources and supports available to help these young people, as well as their friends and families.

The stories contained in each book of this series also contain factual information that will enhance your own understanding of the particular condition being presented. If you or someone you know is struggling with a similar condition or experience, this series can give you important information about where and how you can get help. After reading these stories, we hope that you will be more open to the differences you encounter in your peers and more willing to get to know others who are "different."
—*Carolyn Bridgemohan, M.D.*

Chapter 1
Urban Native

Wham!

Someone shoved Tanya Begay from the back—hard.

She fell face forward onto the dirty sidewalk. Stuff in her purse spilled. Before she realized what happened, Tanya saw her MP3 player fly onto the sidewalk, scooped up instantly by a thin brown hand.

"Hey! Stop! That's mine."

Tanya looked up from the pavement to see a girl her own age, a Latina wearing a tank top and baggy pants, racing down the street.

The girl shouted over her shoulder, "It's mine now!"

And disappeared around a corner.

Tanya turned painfully to sit up on the sidewalk; she could see a dark stain spreading through the right knee of her jeans. *Ooh, blood . . .*

Then her emotions turned to rage. *I worked at Shiprock Gas Station for a year so I could buy that. How can that girl do such a thing? And here I am, bleeding on the sidewalk—and no one even asks if I'm okay. This city sucks the life out of people.*

Just an hour earlier, things had been going along like normal.

The dismissal bell rang and students poured out the doors of Shore View High.

Thank heavens, Tanya thought, *ten more minutes of biology class and I would go raving mad. Every day in this lousy school seems like forever.*

Tanya didn't bother stopping by her locker; she threw her backpack over her shoulders—*feels like a ton of bricks*—and made a beeline for the nearest exit.

"Hey, Tanya! I'm going shopping—want to come with me?"

Tanya turned to look at Vanna Khan, standing beside her locker. Vanna was dressed in a form-fitting red outfit—blouse, jacket, and mini-skirt all matching—with high heels and pink pantyhose. Although she had lived in Huntington Beach for a whole semester, Tanya was still amazed people actually wore clothes like that. She glanced down at her own clothes: a Rez Girl T-shirt with the words "Navajo Forever" and a pair of faded, patched jeans.

Why does she even ask? Making fun of me? I don't have money to go shopping every day like this rich Asian girl does—and she knows it.

"Uh, thanks Vanna. I have to go straight home. Tons of homework tonight."

"Yeah, Mr. Vallencio really piled it on us in biology, huh? Well, anytime you feel like new clothes just say the word. I can show you the coolest boutiques in town. I know 'em like the back of my hand."

"Thanks, Vanna, will do."

Horse manure. What is she trying to tell me? My clothes aren't good enough? Does she think she's doing me a favor? I can just imagine Vanna with her friends: "Let's show some pity for the Indian girl—she's s-o-o clueless when it comes to fashion." No thanks, Vanna. We've been put down and used long enough to know better.

As she stepped outside into the bright California sunlight, another voice hailed her. "Hey, Tanya B. We need help with our booth at the Anaheim Powwow this weekend. Can you help us make fry bread?"

Tanya smiled at George Dark Horse, a senior and president of the school's Native Culture Club. "Hiya, George. I think I can be there; need to double-check with my mom, though. Let ya know tomorrow, okay?"

"Fine. Thanks, Tanya."

"Later."

Culture Club's okay—kids there make more sense than non-Natives at school. But there's only one other Navajo; and most of what the club does is customs from other nations. Pow-wows aren't something I grew up with. I'm not sure I really want to go.

As she held this internal conversation with herself, Tanya continued down the street to the bus stop: she was going to visit her cousin Krystie Yazzy, who lived in LA. Most kids at Shore View were rich and had their own cars; but Tanya didn't mind taking the bus. People on the bus never talk to each other, and she enjoyed having time to herself. It was harder at school, where she had to think what to say to people all the time.

Twenty minutes later, the bus stopped, and Tanya stepped off. The city streets were littered with garbage; walls were covered with graffiti, and the people were a mix of Hispanics, blacks, and Asians—much more diverse than Huntington Beach with its Caucasian majority.

Everyone here assumes I'm Hispanic, Tanya mused to herself. *Back in Arizona, off the Rez, people look down on me 'cause I'm Indian. Here, they look down on me because they think I'm Mexican.*

Caught up in her thoughts, Tanya didn't see a large brick in front of her on the sidewalk. Her tennis shoe caught it and she fell, turning an ankle.

Dang! What was that? Ouch, shoulda looked where I was going.

She walked with a slight limp now, angry and frustrated. She had two more blocks to go to the apartment where Krystie lived with Tanya's aunt Angela. Krystie was Tanya's best friend in Southern California; they had lived close to one another in Navajo Nation and known each other as long as Tanya could recall.

And then, wham! She was shoved, bruised, and ripped off. This was definitely not her day.

Tanya picked up the remaining items from her purse and wearily pulled herself up off the pavement, then hobbled down the street to her cousin's.

Krystie opened the door before Tanya even knocked. "Tanya! What happened?"

"I tripped on something in the middle of the sidewalk, then got mugged."

"Oh, no! Come in, sit down. Let me get some ice. Who did this?"

"Some Mexican. Knocked me over and took my MP3 player."

"That's awful."

"She looked real gangsta."

"We should start a Navajo gang in LA."

"Yeah, right—that would help. We could sink to the level of this whole stinking city."

"Oh Tanya, I'm so sorry." Krystie gave her cousin a hug.

Tanya pulled away from her cousin's comforting arms. "I can't wait till I graduate. Mom said I can decide for myself where to live then, and I know what I'm gonna do. Get on the train and head back to the Rez—the minute I can get outta here!"

Krystie wrinkled her nose. "You're sure? You're having a bad day, but there's lots of cool things to do here that you can't do in Arizona."

"You bet I'm sure. Every day here has been a bad day. I don't fit in—you're my only real friend. It's always noisy. Every night, I can't sleep 'cause of the sirens and all the stereos blasting. Traffic is awful. The air is brown. I want to live where I can have a horse and see clear blue skies and red mesas like where I grew up."

Krystie shook her head. "You're being kind of romantic, Tanya. It's not like home was this perfect place. There was a meth lab just down the street, remember? The chemicals killed everything living around the trailer. And remember when Joey StandsTall shot your dog? You know how many of our friends got pregnant. We had all the same problems there that we have here."

"No, it isn't the same, Krystie. Here, you can't get away from craziness. I remember how Grandpa Peshlaki taught us to live the right way, the beauty way. But how can anyone walk in beauty in the middle of this mess? There's bad influences on the Rez, for sure, but people there can go out in the desert and get away from it." Tanya shook her head. "You can stay here if you want, Krystie, but soon as I can I'm going back home where I belong."

Another full year before I can do that, though, Tanya thought. *How will I stand it? Another day like this one and I'm going crazy. Maybe that's it—have a nervous breakdown, cry and scream, so Mom will have to let me go back to the Rez. Maybe that's my ticket home.*

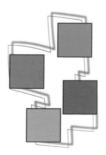

It's About Being Different

How would you feel if there was something about you that made you stand apart from everyone else? It could be anything—something about your hair, the way you talk, the clothes you wear, or what you believe in.

Whatever the source of the difference, it's part of what makes each person in the world unique. For most, these unique qualities are of little consequence. But, for many, the differences are so **profound** they can cause problems fitting in with others. Differences based on one's culture can be the most difficult for others to accept

What Is Culture?

From the time we are born, we are influenced by the world around us, especially by our families. People are born with certain common traits, such as the need to eat and drink. But, *how, when,* and *what* a particular individual eats and drinks are influenced by her culture. The need to consume food and liquid is biologically based. The way those needs are met are learned behaviors, usually based on a person's culture.

But culture goes beyond affecting how biological needs are met. What exactly is meant by the word *culture*? According to *Merriam-Webster's Collegiate Dictionary*, eleventh edition, culture is "the customary beliefs, social forms, and material traits of a racial, religious, or social group . . . the characteristic features of everyday existence . . . shared by people in a place or time." So, it also influences what one watches on television—or even if they have a TV!—what one wears, what someone does for fun, and many more things. There's no getting away from one's culture.

Others' Culture Is All Around Us

What did you have for dinner last night? If you're like many people, you had at least one dish representative of another culture. In many homes, salsa has replaced ketchup as a condiment of choice. Spaghetti and lasagna are favorite dishes in homes and restaurants.

And speaking of restaurants, just take a look in the Yellow Pages in almost any town, and you'll find offerings from many different cultures. Along with fast-food giants Burger King and McDonalds, you're just as likely to find Taco Bell or Taco Grande, as well as full-service Mexican restaurants.

North American sales of chips and salsa are now exceeding that of all-time favorites like white bread and ketchup. This is just one indication of the way minority cultural offerings can become mainstream.

Chapter 2
Surprise Visit

Tap-tap-tap.

It was Saturday afternoon, and Tanya was alone in her room when her mother knocked on the door.

"What is it, Mom?" *Why can't she just leave me alone?*

"What are you doing in there all day?"

"Working on the computer, Mom."

"I thought you were going out with Native Culture Club."

"Nope."

Tanya sighed. *I suppose I could get up and turn the knob—let her in—but she'd probably give me some big lecture; better to talk through the door.*

"Well, it's good you're home anyway. I have a big surprise for you."

"What's that?"

"You'll see."

Tanya heard her mother's footsteps going back down the stairs.

Big surprise: bet it's something lame.

Tanya returned her attention to the laptop positioned on her knees. She was improving her Web site, adding a category titled "Top ten reasons LA sucks." So far, she had entered:

10. Muggers
 9. Traffic never moves
 8. Boys are stuck-up jerks
 7. Smog
 6. People care more what you wear than who you
    really are
 5. Everything costs twice its worth

She was pondering number four when the doorbell rang, and her mom called up the stairs, "Come down. See who's here!"

Tanya sighed again, closed her laptop and set it on the bed, then went downstairs. *What now?*

Her mom stood beaming next to a lanky man with a weathered face, wearing a baseball cap decorated with two eagle feathers.

"Grandpa Peshlaki!"

"*Ya'a'teeh, Nana,*" he called out in a husky but strong voice.

"*Ya'a'teeh,* Gramps. What are you doing in California?"

"Would you believe I came to see my daughter and granddaughter because I miss them so much?"

"No way."

"Yes—it gets lonely for an old man, listening to the coyotes howl and trying to get the satellite dish to pick up more stations in the desert," he said, smiling. "And besides, I was invited by the Museum of Today's Art to display my paintings. Thought I'd do that while I'm here—since I was gonna come see you two anyway."

"Papa, you're going to have an exhibition at MOTA? That's amazing!" exclaimed Tanya's mom.

"Oh, you know these *bilagaana*—they'll pay big bucks for anything Native. I could probably smear horse turds on a canvas and sell it in some gallery."

"Don't be silly," Tanya replied, "You're a great artist, even if being a shaman means you have to be modest and all that. Everyone raves about your paintings. Your art deserves a big show."

Grandpa shrugged. "Now, where should I put these?" He pointed to a pair of duffle bags he had dragged just inside the door.

"Tanya, take Grandpa's things to the guest room, will you please? And Papa, come on in and sit down in the kitchen. I'll get you some iced tea."

A few minutes later, the three of them were sitting around the dining room table. Grandpa said to Tanya's mom, "Lori, it was sad to see you leave when you got the job here, but I can see now it was good for you. You look real good, you have this lovely apartment, and you live in such a fascinating city."

Tanya choked on her iced tea. As soon as she recovered, she blurted, "Yeah, right. Fascinating city—you don't live here."

Her mother shot her a sharp glance, "Is that any way to speak to your elders?"

"Sorry, Mom. Sorry, Gramps."

Her grandfather looked at her for a moment and then asked, "You don't like it here?"

"I hate it. No one understands me. Everything is crowded and expensive. This week a girl pushed me and took my MP3 player. I'm moving back to Navajo Nation soon as I graduate."

"Hmm." Grandpa thought a moment. "Have you tried to make friends here?"

"There's no one for me to be friends with in Huntington Beach. Native people in this town are all from other tribes—real different. This stuck-up rich Asian girl keeps asking me to hang with her, but I think she's just making fun of me. Krystie is my only real friend in California."

"Have you tried kindness with these people, the ones different from you?"

Tanya shrugged. "Either they think I'm Mexican, or if they know I'm Navajo, they act like I'm from some other planet. It's no good. I'm back to the Rez—first moment I can."

Grandpa Peshlaki stared out the window for a minute; he seemed to have tuned out of the conversation, but Tanya knew better. She had seen the elderly healer do this numerous times before, as it was his habit to think before speaking. When he did speak, his words would be weighty, which was why people regarded him so highly as a shaman. Not only had he studied the chants, herbs, and knowledge to become a *haatali*; he also had a reputation for wisdom that outshone his medicinal skills.

Grandpa turned and looked at his granddaughter. "Nana, you are struggling to achieve *hozho* in this place . . . but you don't find harmony. Maybe you have misplaced your focus."

Tanya bit her lip; only Grandpa could speak to her like this—as if she was still a child, needing advice.

"Misplaced my focus, Grandpa?"

"Yes, Nana. To find balance you must be concerned with others. Instead of asking, 'What is in this city for me?' seek ways to bless others around you—people different from yourself."

That's crazy, no way, Tanya thought, biting her lip even harder.

"That's a good idea, Papa." Tanya's mom put a hand on her daughter's shoulder, "I saw an ad for literacy tutors at the public library—maybe you could volunteer for that."

Tanya's head was swirling, but she decided to speak her mind. "But Grandpa, you don't live here—you don't understand. California has all the worst things we have on the reservation, like the medicines that make people crazy and the people with heavy pants who make violence, but that's just part of it. The air makes your lungs burn, and there's crowds of people and noise and traffic jams everywhere, all the time."

Grandpa nodded slightly. "It's not always easy to live the good way—but when you walk in harmony, you can bring light into dark places. Reach out to others. When people are different from one another, they can learn from their differences, while they also come to recognize all that they have in common. Remember, not everyone has been blessed as you have been. There are many who are different here, just as you are, many who do not fit in, but their differences put them at a disadvantage you may not understand. Being truly poor is a difference that is hard to overcome. Stretch yourself. Reach out to those who lack what you have. And by doing so, you may find beauty where you never imagined."

Tanya could feel her heart pounding with anger, but she steeled herself to stay polite. "Thank you Grandpa, I'll think about what you said. But most of all, I'm glad you're here." She gave him a hug, then ran to her room, slammed the door, threw herself in a chair, and put her face in her hands.

Grandpa is a famous artist, a great healer—but he doesn't understand. He lives on the Rez and visits LA every decade or so—so he thinks it's all cool. He didn't get mugged today; he doesn't have to put up with the idiots at school, so he gives me this lame advice, "reach out to others . . . find beauty." Yeah. Right. Sometimes I wonder if I'll even get out of this city alive.

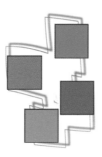

How Is *Someone* Culturally Deprived?

Although culture surrounds people daily, it is still possible to be culturally deprived. If one's immediate world differs significantly from that of others with whom he or she has contact, it might be hard for that person to fit in among peers. For example, if a family's religious beliefs don't allow them to have a television, children in the family may find it difficult, if not impossible, to relate to conversations among friends about the latest episodes of the season's hottest television shows.

When someone differs in this kind of manner, it introduces another definition of the word *culture*: "acquaintance with and taste in fine arts, humanities, and broad aspects of science" (*Merriam-Webster's Collegiate Dictionary*, eleventh edition). Someone not exposed to a community's fine arts, for example, can also be said to be culturally deprived.

Not having a television or lacking exposure to the arts are just two ways someone can be culturally deprived. Most people might think those are relatively minor. But, to the person who might be **ostracized** because of them, it could be an important difference.

There are other forms of cultural deprivation that most people would consider important. The child without a home is certainly culturally deprived. While other children go to their homes after school, children who are homeless may go to a temporary shelter; others may sleep in cars with their families.

This difference puts the children at an enormous disadvantage, as they are not able to have the same experiences as their peers.

Economically deprived children can also be culturally deprived. Children in poverty do not have the same experiences as their **contemporaries**. This can put them socially and academically behind others their own age. This kind of delay can affect them throughout their lives.

Poverty has its own culture, and children born within it often lack the opportunities encountered by those in the mainstream culture. These differences can put them at a disadvantage when they try to find their place in the adult world.

Cultural Deprivation Caused by Lack of Resources

In 2004, 37 million people lived in poverty, an increase of 1.1 million in just one year. Thirteen million of them were children. This wasn't a one-year fluke; the number of people living in poverty has increased for four consecutive years. These must be poverty statistics for an undeveloped Third World country, right? Probably some place in Africa. Wrong. These are the most recent statistics available on poverty in the United States, the last of the world's superpowers.

When Hurricane Katrina hit the Gulf Coast of the United States in late August 2005, Americans could not escape the evidence of this country's hidden population of the economically disadvantaged. While many were able to escape the oncoming storm, many more were forced to stay behind, having no means of transportation or even a place to go. Many of those who died were from this economic class, including ones who perished in hospitals and nursing homes. Although the majority were African American, it was their economic status that many times determined who lived and who died in the storm and its aftermath.

After a visit to the ravaged region, U.S. Senator Barack Obama (D.Ill.) stated:

> There seemed to be a sense that this other America was somehow not on people's radar screen. . . . That is the deeper shame of this past week—that it has taken a crisis like this one to awaken us to the great divide that continues to fester in our midst. That's what all Americans

are truly ashamed about, and the fact that we're ashamed about it is a good sign.

There is a large group of people known as the working poor. They have steady jobs, often more than one. But, despite that, they still have difficulty making ends meet. Many times they can't afford insurance or other protection for themselves and their families. And, if they lose their jobs, their homes can go into **foreclosure**, they can lose their cars, they fall deeper into poverty.

For those in the United States who do not face the possibility of poverty daily, there can be a gross misconception of what poverty means. To some kids,

The majority of those who lost their homes as a result of Hurricane Katrina were economically disadvantaged. Their poverty made them even more vulnerable to trauma and ongoing hardship during the nation's long recovery from this disaster.

poverty means not being able to get the newest PlayStation® game or the latest and hottest style in sneakers. There is little real understanding of what it means to not know what—if anything—there will be to eat. People who do not live this way often find it difficult to *empathize* with those who do.

The poverty line is the income threshold below which one could not afford to buy the things necessary to live. In 2005, the U.S. government set the poverty line at $19,350 for a family of four living in the forty-eight *contiguous* states and the District of Columbia. The poverty line for the same family structure was $24,190 in Alaska and $22,260 in Hawaii.

Determining Poverty in Canada

As in the United States, the government of Canada has a method of determining who lives in poverty. The low-income cut-off (LICO) scale is Canada's

FAST FACTS

The internationally defined poverty level is living on less than US$2 a day. In 2005, more than half the world's population fell below that benchmark. One in five people around the world live on less than $1 a day; that's one billion human beings.

most often used method for determining poverty. Unlike methods used in the United States, however, the LICO factors in the population of the area of residence when calculating who lives in poverty. The LICO represents the number of Canadians who spend 20 percent more of their *gross income* on the basic necessities of food, shelter, and clothing than spent by the average Canadian living in the same area. As might be expected, living in a more populated area requires more money to meet a family's basic needs, so the income amount below which someone is considered to live in poverty is higher in populous areas. A 2001 survey by Statistics Canada found that the average Canadian spent 35 percent of their gross income on food, shelter, and clothing. So, for a family to be counted among those living in poverty, it must spend 55 percent of its before-tax income on the same necessities. In 2004, the LICO-determined poverty cutoffs were:

Before-Tax Low-Income Cut-Offs, 2005

Family Size	Population of Community of Residence				
	500,000 +	100,000-499,999	30,000-99,999	Less than 30,000*	Rural
1	$20,778	$17,895	$17,784	$16,273	$14,303
2	$25,867	$22,276	$22,139	$20,257	$17,807
3	$31,801	$27,386	$27,217	$24,904	$21,891
4	$38,610	$33,251	$33,046	$30,238	$26,579
5	$43,791	$37,711	$37,480	$34,295	$30,145
6	49,389	$42,533	$42,271	$38,679	$33,999
7+	$54,987	$47,354	$47,063	$43,063	$37,853

*Includes cities with a population between 15,000 and 30,000, and small urban areas (under 15,000).

Source: Prepared by the Canadian Council on Social Development using Statistics Canada's Low Income Cut-Offs, from Low Income Cut-Offs for 2004 and Low Income Measures for 2002.

According to Statistics Canada, the total population of that country in 2004 was 31,974,400. Of that number, 3,479,000—11.2 percent—lived in poverty. Of those, 865,000 were children under the age of eighteen.

Some people in Canada are not satisfied with using the LICO to determine poverty level, and in fact, Statistics Canada, who compiles the figures, reports that the numbers represent income inequality, not poverty levels.

The Canadian government is sponsoring an *initiative* to create a needs-based measure of poverty called the Market Basket Measure to replace the LICO. According to Statistics Canada, the poverty line would be determined by how much money would be needed to buy a "basket" of market-priced basic goods and services.

FAST FACT

According to the international organization Save the Children, in 2004, Canada had the world's second-highest rate of child poverty in the industrialized world. Who had the dubious honor of being number one? The United States, with one in six children living below the poverty line.

Other Ways of Determining Who Lives in Poverty

The methods used by the United States and Canada are not the only ones used to determine poverty levels.

- The World Bank uses a method similar to the proposed Market Basket Measure to determine poverty levels on an international scale. To aid in the understanding of poverty levels across countries, it is necessary to have a common currency. The World Bank established Purchasing Power Parity dollars ($PPP) to accomplish this comparison. The $PPP are used to estimate how much it will cost to buy the goods and services necessary to sustain life in different countries.

- To measure relative poverty, the Organization of Economic Cooperation and Development (OECD), another international group, compiles all of a country's net incomes and computes that nation's after-tax median income. People earning less than half of that income are considered to be living in poverty.

Who Are the Children Living in Poverty?

The National Center for Children in Poverty (NCCP) reported in 2005 that approximately 17 percent of

Being poor affects nearly every aspect of a child's life: what she eats, how much sleep she gets, her health, her educational opportunities, her social life, how she talks, and how she dresses. These cultural differences often make it difficult for her to fit in with others her own age.

children in the United States live in poverty. At 30 percent, Washington, D.C., had the highest child poverty rate, followed by the state of Louisiana with 13 percent. Of the ten states with the highest rates of extreme child poverty (with an income less than half of the poverty level), seven of them were in the South. The NCCP also found that black and Latino children were the most likely to live in poverty:

- 33 percent of black children live in poor families. In the ten most populated states, rates of child poverty among black children range from 22 percent in New Jersey to 44 percent in Illinois.

- 28 percent of Latino children live in poor families. In the ten most populated states, rates of child poverty among Latino children range from 17 percent in Michigan to 35 percent in New York and Texas.

- 10 percent of white children live in poor families. In the ten most populated states, rates of child poverty among white children range from 4 percent in New Jersey to 10 percent in Georgia, Michigan, New York, Ohio, and Pennsylvania.

- Although black and Latino children are disproportionately likely to be poor, white children comprise the largest group of children living in poor families—35 percent of all poor children are white.

In Canada, *Aboriginal* children are more likely to live in poverty than their non-Aboriginal peers. The poverty rate of Aboriginal children living in large cities is far greater than of those living in other off-reservation locations. For example, according to Build up Bethlehem, Build up Hope (www.cbmin.org), 72 percent of Aboriginal children living in Winnipeg fall below the poverty line.

Poverty is not restricted to urban areas. In their study of rural poverty, the U.S. Department of Agriculture Economic Research Service (ERS) divides the country into metro (urban) and nonmetro (rural) areas. Nonmetro counties comprise the largest percentage (89 percent) of persistent poverty counties, areas where at least 20 percent of the population was poor over the last thirty years. Most of the nonmetro persistent poverty counties (280) were in the southern United States. There were sixty such counties located in the West and Midwest; there were none in the Northeast.

According to ERS studies, in 2002, 14.2 percent of the U.S. nonmetro population (7.5 million people) lived in poverty. The total can be broken into racial categories:

non-Hispanic Blacks	33 percent
Native Americans	35 percent
non-Hispanic Whites	11 percent
Hispanics	27 percent

More than 50 percent of Native Americans who live in nonmetro areas are classified as being extremely poor.

The Effects of Poverty on Children

When fitting in means the most, coming from impoverished conditions can make school—and life— seem almost unbearable. While peers are talking about the latest electronic gadget, the teen from a poor family may have trouble relating to and participating in the conversation. As much as someone might want to fit in, it can be hard to get excited about an iPod® when you go to bed hungry every night. And following the latest in clothing trends is probably impossible. All of this helps to keep the impoverished child on the outside of healthy social circles.

Children living in poverty can seldom conform to the latest fashion trends!

A person who grows up in poverty may feel as though he faces a world of locked doors. His opportunities are not only limited by financial challenges but by cultural ones as well.

Being poor affects more than just the ability (or inability) to obtain material things. Education can be one way out of poverty, but, unfortunately, coming from a poor family can make getting a good education difficult.

Poor families can be highly mobile, moving from place to place, looking for work or avoiding responsibilities such as paying rent. This often requires changing schools many times within an academic year. The student who frequently changes schools may eventually give up on trying to make friends and getting involved in school activities. Such students may become loners; some may exhibit hostility toward people and property.

Children living in poverty may form their own social networks. While these can contribute to their psychological health, these children will often still face many difficulties trying to interact in the mainstream world at school.

School attendance in general may be *sporadic*. The student might be expected to help earn an income; to the struggling family, this might be seen as more important than receiving an education. If there is a preschool child at home, it may be necessary for the older one to provide child care while a parent works.

Whatever the reason for irregular attendance, it makes it difficult to make and keep friends. It also means that the student may have problems keeping up academically with the rest of the class. Sadly, this can prove detrimental to receiving a good education and leaving behind a life of poverty.

Frequent moves and sporadic attendance also mean that *mandated reporters* of child abuse and neglect might not become aware of these dangerous, potentially life-threatening conditions. With no one to turn to, and no one who knows her well enough to know something is wrong, the student may feel abandoned, left to deal with matters on her own.

Programs That Help

There is help available to children and their families who find themselves living in poverty. Programs such as Head Start help the youngest children get a foot up on the educational and socialization ladder. Most communities have free or reduced-price school lunch programs; some schools have a breakfast program as well. Some school districts also offer breakfast or lunch programs during summer vacation, but with extremely tight budgets, some programs have had to close.

Nonmetro students, particularly those from low-income families, can find it difficult to participate in after-school programs because of a lack of transportation. Some school districts have a late-running school bus so these students can participate, thereby forming the relationships others their age have the ability to make. And programs such as violin lessons provided to low-income students in the Harlem section of New York City by the Opus 118 Music Center, highlighted in the documentary *Small Wonders* and the film *Music of the Heart*, brings

Sometimes, something as seemingly simple as a school bus can make a huge difference in a child's life.

music to students whose families cannot afford to purchase an instrument or pay for lessons.

Child-care programs for low-income families are also available in many areas. Some have early drop-off and late pick-up hours to accommodate parents' work schedules, taking responsibility for the care of younger siblings away from the student.

Unfortunately, many schools and other programs have been forced to cancel or at least curtail many services beneficial to those living in poverty. Some religious-based and other charitable organizations

Children raised in poverty need to be given opportunities to reach beyond their cultural limitations.

have stepped in to provide some of the most-needed services.

Poverty has perhaps one of the most lasting influences on the development of successful children. "The cycle of poverty" is a cliché, but the thing about clichés is that they are based on truth. It is important that children raised in poverty be given the opportunity to break free of that cycle. That includes educational opportunities certainly, but they also need the chance to develop the social skills necessary to a successful and happy life.

Chapter 3
Nura

All right Grandpa, Tanya thought, *I called the literacy program, volunteered to tutor, and here I am—at the 8th Street Library. I could have volunteered in Huntington Beach, but instead I chose this downtown branch, near Krystie's place . . . so now I'm really gonna experience the city.*

Tanya walked past the front desk and knocked on a door that read, "Los Angeles Learns: Literacy Volunteers."

"Come in."

Tanya opened the door and greeted Gloria Gonzales, the coordinator for the program. Gloria wore a perpetual smile, along with dresses that Tanya thought were too bright and too tight, but she appreciated the way Ms. Gonzales radiated optimism.

"So Tanya . . . all trained and ready to begin helping someone?"

"Yes, Ms. Gonzales."

"Very good. Your student is already here—she's a girl your own age, an immigrant from Afghanistan. She's only been in our country four months. The local school has no program designed for Afghans, so you'll need to help supplement her school education."

"Afghanistan? I thought we beat the Taliban over there. Put in democracy and all that. So why are immigrants from there coming here?"

"From what I understand, Nura's family was put on a death list by their local warlord. The warlords aren't Taliban—but they're not exactly democratic either. Nura lived two years in a refugee camp in Pakistan before coming here."

Ms. Gonzales led Tanya through the book stacks to a desk in the back of the library, where Tanya saw a thin girl, with pale skin and brown eyes cast toward the ground, wearing a faded dress that reached all the way to the floor, and a pink scarf wrapped around her head.

Whoa! She looks more out of place in this city than I do, Tanya reflected silently.

"Hello, Nura? I'm your tutor, Tanya Begay."

The girl nodded ever so slightly, neither speaking nor lifting her eyes off the floor.

"So now I'll leave you two alone to get started," said Ms. Gonzales in her upbeat tone, and she spun on her high heels, then headed back toward her office.

Tanya felt panic creep up her spine.

I need to establish contact with this girl somehow. But how?

She pulled up a chair, sat next to Nura, and forced her biggest smile.

"So . . . I hear you're originally from Afghanistan?"

The head beneath the scarf nodded slightly.

"Then you were in Pakistan?"

Again, a slight nod.

"You have family?"

Another slight movement, but no speech yet.

"Do you have brothers or sisters?"

Yet again, a small motion of Nura's head was the only response.

"What are their names?"

Nura didn't answer, but Tanya waited, still smiling.

And waited. . .

Finally, she could stand the silence no longer. "You have sisters?"

A tiny nod yet again.

"How many sisters do you have?"

The girl lifted her hand and raised two fingers.

"Two sisters? That's nice. What are their names?"

Tanya was actually surprised when Nura said, "Sisters . . . names?"

"Yes, that's right. What are your sisters' names?"

"Why . . . why you want to know?" Nura's eyes were wide, her mouth pinched tight.

Tanya sensed more fear than rudeness in the response. "I want to get acquainted, you know . . . uh, I want to get to know you."

The girl's expression seemed to relax infinitesimally. Then the Afghan girl asked, "You . . . have family?"

Now we're making progress. "Yes," Tanya said, "but I'm an only child. No brother, no sister, just me and my mom."

Nura's eyes widened. "No have brother?"

Tanya shook her head.

"No have sister?"

"Just me and my mom."

"No . . . no father?" Nura's voice was incredulous.

"Dad was a deadbeat, so—no father."

"No father . . . dead?" Nura's looked up at Tanya again, her eyes full of questions.

Tanya shook her head. "Not really dead. He just left."

Nura's forehead wrinkled. "You make joke?"

Tanya felt suddenly sad inside. She was just beginning to communicate with this girl and she already disliked the conversation.

"No father . . . no joke. He left us. So there's just my mom and me." Then she added, "But I have a friend—Krystie. She lives close to here. Do you have friends, friends from school?"

Nura's eyes went back to the floor, and she seemed to shrink back slightly. She shook her head.

Shoot. Wrong question.

"Well, I guess we should get to work on your lessons. Is there some school project you need help with?"

The silence this time seemed to last forever. Finally, Tanya said, "Would you like help with reading or writing?"

Nura gave one of her tiny nods.

"Writing?"

Another nod.

"Okay, is there something you're working on at school?"

"Name."

"Huh?"

"Write my name . . . English."

It took a moment for Tanya to realize: *She's been here four months—and she still can't write her name. What are the teachers doing at her school? This girl really does need help.*

"Nura, did you go to school in Afghanistan?"

Nura shook her head. "Taliban . . . girls, no school. Pakistan camp . . . need work. No time school."

She's my age, and never been educated at all. Tanya's mind was boggled.

"All right, Nura. Show me what you've learned here, in the States." She handed the girl a piece of lined paper and a pen.

Nura took the pen hesitantly, as though she thought it might bite her. Then she methodically made three straight lines, a big "N" on the paper. She set down the pen and glanced at Tanya for approval.

Tanya made herself smile. "That's a good start, Nura. N—the first letter of your name. Now let's work on the other three letters."

Tanya was about to form a "u" on the paper when she overheard voices coming from behind a bookshelf a few feet away.

"Country's turning to crap, man—look at that. A wetback and an A-rab. Stupid welfare hos, taking tax money from real Americans. If they're so poor, they should just stay in their own country, not bring their stinking ignorance here."

Tanya felt her heart beat so hard she thought it might burst. She turned to Nura. "Excuse me, I'll be right back."

She stepped to the end of an aisle where she saw two tall white men in their twenties with shaved heads.

"Excuse me," Tanya said, a little too loudly for the library.

They looked down at her in a way that made Tanya squirm.

"Hey, it's the Mexican honey. Come with us and we'll show ya what real men are made of."

Tanya took a deep breath. "I'm *not* your honey, I'm *not* Hispanic, and I *don't* have loose morals. This is a public library, I'm a tutor with the Los Angeles Learns program, and if you don't stop harassing us, I'm going to call security and have you removed."

The two men laughed. One made an obscene gesture, while the other shrugged. Then they both turned and walked away, as though she were too small and dirty for them to look at any longer.

But as they walked past the desk where Nura sat, one of the men grabbed her shoulder, turning the Afghan girl toward him. "We don't need no effin' A-rabs, you hear me towel-head? Just get out of our country, and go back to your own stinkin' part of the world."

His companion laughed, and the two hastened out of the library.

Oh God, I hope she didn't understand all that, Tanya begged silently. But Nura had. When Tanya sat back down beside the other girl, she saw tears glistening on Nura's cheeks.

Nura spoke quietly. "I am not Arab. I am Pashtun." Her voice choked; she swallowed and whispered, "My people are good . . . serve Allah, live . . . old ways . . . don't hurt anyone. Why people hate me?"

Suddenly, Tanya felt water pouring out of her own tear ducts. This girl, outwardly so strange and different from herself, seemed all at once to be kin. Tanya put her hand gently on Nura's arm. The Afghan girl tensed, but she didn't move away. She lifted her glistening eyes toward Tanya's face, and for the first time the two girls looked eye-to-eye.

"Nura," Tanya spoke slowly, enunciating her words, filling each syllable with earnestness. "I know how you feel. I'm a Navajo Indian, and we also try to live the good way, but sometimes people treat us bad too, because they are prejudiced, and ignorant."

She looked at the girls' eyes. *Does she understand?* Tanya wasn't sure.

"Nura, I want to stand by you."

Still no sign of understanding.

"I will help you."

Tanya struggled to find the words that would communicate what she meant. "I want to be your friend."

For the first time, Tanya saw a slight smile form on Nura's lips.

"You . . . friend for Nura?"

This time, it was Tanya's turn to nod.

"Thank you, Tan-ya Buh-gay. I need a friend."

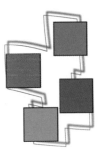

Immigrant Children and Children of Immigrants

Give me your tired, your poor,
Your huddled masses yearning to breathe free,
The wretched refuse of your teeming shore.
Send these, the homeless, tempest-tossed, to me:
I lift my lamp beside the golden door.

These words are inscribed on a plaque at the foot of the Statue of Liberty, one of the best-known symbols of freedom in the world. For many years, immigrants have been coming to the United States in search of that freedom, in search of a new and better life

According to the U.S. Office of Immigration Statistics (OIS), in 2005, a total of 1,122,373 immigrants applied for **permanent resident** status. The largest percentage (161,445) were from Mexico. Americans have opened their families to the adoption of immigrant orphans as well. The OIS reports that Americans adopted 22,710 foreign-born children in 2005.

Canada has also been a destination point for immigrants from around the world. According to Statistics Canada, 5,448,480 people moved to Canada in 2001. The largest percentage of the immigrants came from Southeast Asia (730,600), followed closely by southern Europe (715,370).

What does that mean? Put simply, there are a lot of people in the United States and Canada whose **ethnicity**, customs, and appearance differ from those of the majority in the United States and Canada. Two of the biggest challenges facing immigrants and the children of immigrants are language and stereotypes. With those differences can come difficulty in adjusting to life in a new country.

The Statue of Liberty continues to be a symbol of opportunity for immigrants—but many of the young people who come to North America also face difficult challenges.

Language

One of the most serious and immediate problem areas for immigrants is language. Imagine being in a store and unable to make anyone understand what you're trying to find. That would be frustrating, right? But, what if you or someone in your family needed emergency medical assistance and the same thing happened? No matter what you did, you just couldn't get anyone to understand what was wrong and what kind of help you needed. The inability to have this type of communication understood could cost someone his or her life. Well, that is the reality faced by many immigrants to the United States and Canada.

If an immigrant child comes to the United States before she has acquired her own language, she might still learn her native language first. After all, that will probably be the language spoken in the home, where she will learn to talk. However, it is likely that the child will also pick up English in the course of her everyday life as well. This can ease transition into school, alleviating one problem faced by immigrant students.

This is not always the case, though. According to a 2002 story in the *Washington Post*, 35 percent of students in English for Speakers of Other Languages (ESOL) classes are U.S. citizens. These students are the U.S.-born children of immigrants. In many cases, their families are poor, and their parents have little education and are employed for long hours at low-paying jobs. The children may spend many hours alone, with little exposure to other people or U.S.

culture. They and their families are isolated. In the past, immigrant communities would spring up in a city, such as Chinatown or the Little Italy sections of New York City. More recent immigration trends, however, have seen the scattering of immigrants all across the United States. Rather than cultural **enclaves** that can fill in for the parents, families can be left to fend for themselves. The result, according to the *Post* story, is that these children have little knowledge of their own language or of English. Some teachers in the suburban Washington, D.C., area report that this can make learning English more difficult for these

San Francisco has one of North America's largest and oldest Chinatowns. Modern-day immigrants, however, are more apt to scatter throughout North America, rather than settle in their own communities.

students than it was for immigrants in the past.

Some researchers have expressed a concern that Mexicans immigrating to the Southwest may be learning English too slowly, thereby hindering their *assimilation* into the U.S. mainstream. Harvard University professor Samuel P. Huntington has stated that this slowness to learn English is leading to a separatist threat to mainstream culture. Some compare this to the situation of the French-speaking province of Quebec in Canada, which has proposed that it secede from Canada. Most research has shown, however, that as of the 2005 Census, 71 percent of Latino children of immigrants and 89 percent of Asian children of immigrants speak English very well

Many Latino children grow up hearing Spanish spoken as the first language in their homes. This may put them at a disadvantage in school setting where instruction, books, and tests are all provided in English.

FAST FACT

What's the difference between immigrant children and children of immigrants? An immigrant child is one who was born in a foreign country and moved to another one, such as Canada or the United States. Children of immigrants are born in the United States or Canada, for example, of parents who immigrated there. Unlike their parents—who may or may not be citizens, who may or may not be in the country legally— according to U.S. law, all children of immigrants are considered U.S. citizens with all of the rights and responsibilities that go along with it.

or only speak English in their homes. Among **second-generation immigrants** in Miami, Florida, and San Diego, California, researchers in 2001 reported that by their senior year in high school, 98 percent spoke and understood English well or very well, though most used their parents' native language at home.

Though the ability to speak English will benefit the immigrant children, it can also cause additional stress on them, especially as they get older. While it is possible to learn another language at any age, younger people almost always find it easier to do so. In some cases, adults never achieve a working

Teenagers in immigrant families may feel responsible for helping their parents cope with an alien culture.

knowledge of English. Instead, their children become personal translators, helping their parents with everyday tasks. While other teens are playing sports, going to parties, or just having other types of fun, translator-children are assuming part of the role of adult. They must go with their parents to doctor's appointments and pharmacies, to stores, to banks, even to attorneys' offices when there are legal matters with which to deal. For many of these children, this has been a part of their lives for a very long time, and will continue to be one of their responsibilities for many years to come. Even the choice of a college or job may be influenced by the need to stay in the vicinity of their parents so they can continue to help their parents cope with the language barrier.

Stereotypes

After al-Qaeda terrorists attacked the United States in 2001, government officials, celebrities, and others hurried to plead with the public not to take out its anger on the Muslim population as a whole. There was a fear that a few Americans might believe that all Muslims shared the beliefs of the terrorists on the planes and harm innocent people. Though there were some scattered incidents of hate crimes toward Muslims, including some that ended with deaths, most Americans did not fall into the stereotype trap.

Stereotypes—oversimplified standardized images or ideas held by one person or group about another, often based on incomplete and inaccurate information—may be the most difficult battle immigrant children and children of immigrants must

> # *FAST FACT*
>
> *A frequently heard argument of the past against having a woman president concerned the famous red "hotline" phone on the president's desk. Some believed that a woman would be too emotional to handle a nuclear crisis or any kind of national threat if it occurred during her menstrual cycle. Talk about stereotypes!*

face. Other problems, including language, can be dealt with directly by the children. Though it might not be easy, especially if the native language has a completely different alphabet, new languages can be learned—at any age. However, when dealing with stereotypes, one is confronted with the prejudice caused by ideas and beliefs of someone else.

All Mexicans are lazy. All Muslims are fanatics who think the United States is evil. All French people smell bad. Those are all common stereotypes. But, so are: all blacks have rhythm, all Italians belong to the Mafia, all Irish are drunkards and hotheads, and all women are too emotional to hold positions of power. Thankfully, those last stereotypes have faded from the memories of most people. Though they seem ridiculous now, all were commonly held beliefs during different points in our history. Let's hope that the other stereotypes disappear as well.

Some stereotypes may not seem harmful or negative at all. For example, "All Japanese are good at math, computers, and electronics." Some people may even think that they are giving a compliment when they say things like that. Well, what if you're Japanese and, because your interests lie elsewhere, you've not given much thought or developed skills in those areas? If the child doesn't fit into that pigeonhole, she may feel inadequate, unworthy, no matter the intention of the speaker.

Stereotypes emphasize differences, usually the ones that will make one group feel that they are better than another. As with anything that describes how one person is not like another, this has an isolating effect. A recent immigrant from a Muslim country may be looked upon by other students in the class as a potential terrorist. Students may assume that the new kid in the class from Mexico crossed the border in the middle of the night and is here illegally. And stereotypes about students are not necessarily limited to the other young members of the class. An overworked teacher may be relieved when he learns that a transfer student from Japan will be in his computer class. After all, the teacher might believe, she won't need much help.

Chapter 4
Angela

Several weeks later, Tanya was disembarking from the bus en route to the library for another appointment with Nura.

Things are going better than I expected, she reflected as she strode down the sidewalk.

Nura had opened up since their initial meeting, and the two girls spoke freely now about their homes, their lives, and their dreams. She was also proving to be a gifted pupil, quickly advancing from the English alphabet to the point where she could write entire sentences.

Tanya was so caught up in her thoughts that she walked right into someone. . . .

It's the girl that took my MP3 player!

Tanya blurted, "It's you! You shoved me—you took my—"

"Quiet, *puta,* or I'll off ya right here."

Tanya felt something cold and sharp shove against her stomach. She glanced down. Held tightly in the other girl's hand was a knife.

The girl's voice was husky. "You wanna mess with me, *chola?* Wanna piece of me?"

Tanya looked at her adversary, appraising her. The girl was all attitude: baggy pants barely hanging on her wide hips, a white strapless top with bra-straps protruding onto her shoulders, arms covered with tattoos. She wore a blue handkerchief tied around her right thigh, showing her colors. The girls' stomach bulged; this fierce creature was pregnant? Tanya looked into her black-rimmed eyes, and they glared back defiantly.

Tanya caught her breath and spoke quietly, trying to appear calm. "I'm not looking for trouble."

"You talkin' trash 'bout I stole something from you. I'll cutcha."

Tanya took another breath, *Good Spirits, help me now.* "I don't want to fight you. I don't have a gun or a knife, and I wouldn't hurt you if I did."

The other girl remained tense, the knife still pressing against Tanya's skin. "What's your flag, *chola?* Florencia?"

Tanya shook her head.

"Eighth Street?"

"No."

"Blood?"

"No."

"Don't mess with me, *puta*."

"I'm not messing with you."

"Then what's this smack talk 'bout me pushin' you?"

Tanya hesitated; she realized a wrong word could be her last. On the other hand, she thought, *May as well be forthright—at least I'll meet Creator with my last words being honest ones.* "I'm not part of a gang. I'm not Latina, either. I'm Navajo."

"What? You on crack, girl? Never heard of that gang."

"I told you, I'm not in a gang. I'm an American Indian."

Tanya felt the knife pull away from her stomach.

"Indian—like Geronimo?"

"Well, no, not exactly. I'm Navajo. Geronimo was Apache."

The other girl's eyes flicked over Tanya. "You live in a tepee?"

I don't believe this. She's threatening my life, and I've got to explain away these old cultural stereotypes? Tanya sighed.

"We used to live in hogans—eight-sided homes made from logs and earth. But nowadays those are mostly used for ceremonies on the reservation. My mom and I live in a condo in Huntington Beach."

The girl's eyes narrowed. "I see Apaches in the movies on TV. You guys are tough. Think you can take me?"

This girl doesn't hear things very well, does she? "I told you, I'm not Apache, and I don't want a fight. I don't want trouble."

"So, *chica*—what *do* you want?"

Should leave well enough alone, get out of here in one piece, Tanya told herself, but she still felt aggrieved about the stolen MP3 player. "I want to know what you were thinking when you knocked me down and took my player. I worked hard—a long time—to buy that."

"Sure. You probably jacked it."

"No, I worked at the Shiprock Gas Station and I earned it."

"Ship rock? Never heard of it. What hood you from?"

"No hood. I was raised in Navajo Nation, in Arizona." *And I wish I was still there right now.*

"Listen, chola, this ain't the place to talk. Step into the alley there, *comprendes?*"

Oh no, she's gonna rob me again—or maybe attack me. But she had the knife so Tanya decided to do what the girl said. Her skin crawled up and down her arms, and her heart pounded.

But after they stepped into the alley, to Tanya's delighted surprise, the other girl folded her knife and slipped it into a pocket.

"I ride with 13th Street. My G name is *La Loca*." She added more quietly, "But my real name is Angela."

Tanya nodded, waited. *What's going on?* she asked silently. *Why are you telling me this?*

Angela continued, even more quietly, as if afraid someone was listening, "You and me, we got something in common."

That's a joke, Tanya thought.

But the girl continued. "*Mi familia* came here from Guatemala. There, we were *indigena*—like you are."

Tanya's eyes widened. She looked more closely at the girl's cheekbones, her thick black hair; for the second time that year, Tanya felt a surprising sense of kinship.

"Angela, we Navajos know that part of our tribe journeyed to the south, to the land of endless summer, a long time ago. You . . . you could actually be my distant cousin."

Angela's eyes grew wide. "My people, we called ourselves Jaguar Clan. We have the same story, about the people who stayed in *el Norte* a long time ago."

Tanya and Angela eyed each other, hovering on the boundary line between distrust and friendship. Then Angela said, "The other folks in Guatemala—the *Ladinos*—they put us down for being *indigenas*. They think we're all stupid, dirty—but we had pride. My uncle, Ramón, he was a shaman—that's kind of like a *curandero*, ya know? He'd do magic."

Tanya was now truly astonished. "My Grandpa Pesh-laki, he's a singer—a *haatali*. It's kind of the same thing."

"Really?"

"For real."

"Wow. So . . . one day, Ramón he made sacrifices like he does with the *copal* and a chicken. And he saw stuff, like shamans do. He saw in his mind that some people were going to come to our *casa* and destroy it, so they could make farms for the rich people from *Ciudad Guatemala*. So he tells us, 'Better go now. Go to *El Norte*. There's gonna be no way to live here.' So we got on a bus, and drove all up through Mexico."

It was hard to believe, this girl that had been poking her with a deadly weapon was now, just five minutes later, pouring out her life story. Tanya found herself both fascinated and amazed by Angela.

"How did you get across the border?" Tanya asked the other girl. "Did you have immigration papers?"

"You on crack, *chola*? We were *pobres indios*. We didn't have *nada* in Guatemala."

"So. . . ?"

"So we get off the bus in Sonora and hook up with *el coyote* to get us across the border. But we didn't have nothing to pay the guy, but my brother Jorge, he broke into a store at night and got some money, so we quick paid *el coyote*, and then he led us across the desert. Aye! It was effin' hot, like an oven. We were so thirsty. . . ." Angela's voice faded away.

But I can wait, Tanya thought. *If it's one thing we Diné understand, it's the way sometimes you have to be quiet before something unfolds.*

Angela continued, more slowly now "Papá, he got bit . . . by a great big rattlesnake. Jorge killed it with his machete, but Papá's leg swelled up real big. The *coyote*—he just runs off and leaves Papá to die." Angela was silent again for a long moment. "Then the rest of us, Mamá, Jorge, my sister Lupita and me, we kept going. Our legs hurt . . . our insides felt like they were full of sharp rocks . . . but we made it to Tucson. Then we called some relatives in LA and they sent money for the bus   and now this is home."

"You're a long way from Guatemala, huh?"

"This is home now, girl . . . what did you say your name was?"

Tanya extended her hand gingerly, "Tanya Begay. Pleased to meet you, Angela."

"Uh, yeah." The other girl didn't take the offered hand, but she didn't seem offended either.

Tanya decided to risk a question. "Are you . . . expecting a baby, Angela?"

"Yeah. I'm knocked up."

"Married?"

"Nah, it's my homeboy G-Dog, but he's in the slammer."

Tanya decided to change the subject. "Angela . . . how did you get involved with a gang?"

There was an awkward silence, and Tanya could see the Guatemalan girl's brow wrinkle, as if she were searching through the dark attics of her soul.

"My sister Lupita, she made friends here pretty quick, but she got onto meth and needed more and more of it, so she made some bad deals. One day, this guy got all mad at her because she owed him money and she couldn't pay." Angela paused and took a deep breath. "That *vato*, man, he smoked her, just pulled out his tool and smoked her, 'bang!' just like that . . . just 'cause she couldn't pay him for that stupid meth."

Tanya didn't know what to say. "I'm sorry." The words didn't seem strong enough or big enough.

"Yeah, well . . . the guy that did it, he was ridin' with the Florencias. I knew some gangstas, they were 13th Street, and they come to me and say, 'That G-boy that smoked your *hermana*, it's time he gets knocked.' And I tell 'em, 'Word,' and they say, 'We can get that *cholo* . . . we can smoke him. But we need you to jump in.' So I told them, 'I'm down with that.' I jumped in—and we had a shovel party for that *vato*."

Tanya felt a chill. "Don't you ever want out of the gang?"

Angela laughed. "You *are* on crack. I jump out, the Florencias do me. It's ride or die, *chica*."

Tanya shook her head, but Angela just shrugged her shoulders.

"Hey, I've gotta go." Angela began to leave the alley, then turned and walked back.

Now what? Tanya thought, bracing herself.

Angela stuck her hand deep into the pocket of her baggy black pants. Tanya wondered if she was going for the knife again.

But Angela's hand emerged with Tanya's MP3 player.

"Hey, I jacked this offa some Apache chick. Think maybe you should have it."

"Uh, thanks," Tanya stuttered, "uh, Navajo not Apache."

"Whatever. Nice meeting you . . . cuz."

Angela disappeared around the corner of the alley, and Tanya leaned back against the wall, exhausted by the swirl of emotions she had just experienced.

She looked down at the MP3 player in her hand. *I never thought I'd talk to the girl who took this. And I thought my life was rough! I feel so sorry for her—but at the same time, she scares me. She's like a wounded cougar: fascinating but dangerous.*

Illegal Immigrants

The United States is faced with the increasing problem of illegal immigration, and by a lack of **consensus** about what should be done to deal with it. There is a clearly defined procedure for entering the United States. Some, however, choose to enter the country without the proper paperwork. For some, it's a matter of a lack of money, for others it takes too long. Whatever the reason for **circumventing** the rules, illegal immigration is a political and social issue in which no one will come out a clear winner.

Children who enter the United States with parents who are illegal immigrants are unlikely to find the same opportunities that other children have at school and in the community.

Not all illegal immigrants came to this country illegally, crossing the Texas border on foot under cover of night or in the back of vans. Many came to this country legally but overstayed the limits on their *visas*.

Children born in the United States of illegal immigrants are citizens of this country. They don't have to worry about immigration authorities— well, at least not coming after them specifically. However, whether legally American citizens or illegal immigrants, children *will* worry about their parents. Because they fear that authorities will send them back to their home countries, many illegal immigrants and their families try to "stay under the radar" as much as possible. Some become migrant farmworkers, traveling to wherever the crops are. Others take low-paying, menial jobs, leading to a life in poverty.

Poverty and frequent moves brought on by illegal immigration status can make it difficult for a student to receive an education. Even students living in more permanent locations may encounter difficulties getting an education. Accurate birth certificates and school records may be unavailable. Many find parent–teacher conferences something to be avoided, especially when the parents do not speak English, as many illegal immigrants do not. This can mean that the student will not receive the help needed to achieve academic success, a key to escaping the cycle of poverty.

Fear of being reported to immigration authorities may also prevent illegal immigrant families from receiving medical care. Children who do not receive vaccinations, as can be the case under these circumstances, are susceptible to easily preventable childhood illnesses that can affect them for the rest of their lives.

Perhaps almost as feared as being reported to authorities is the fear of the "coyote," the person paid to smuggle them across the border in the case of illegal immigrants from Mexico, or the person who provided them with counterfeit papers—for a price of course—for illegal immigrants from other countries. Children and their parents can live in fear of reprisals should they not be able to make their payments on

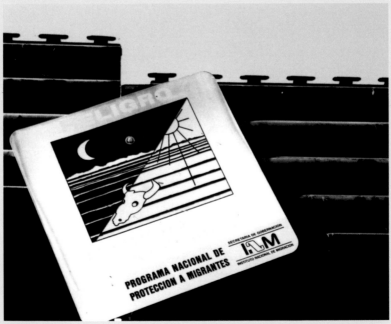

Crossing the border from Mexico into the United States is often a dangerous journey for illegal immigrants.

time. There have been cases in which children have been kidnapped and held until past due payments were made current. But again, the fear of being "sent back" often overrides the fear of harm, even death. In most cases, these incidents, and other cases of violence, go unreported.

The True Native Populations

By no one's definition should the Native Americans of the United States or Canada's First Nations be considered an immigrant population. However, children of Native populations can face many of the same problems as immigrants.

Many Native Americans and First Nations peoples live on reservations, segregated from the mainstream, like some immigrant families. Those who do choose to live off the reservation often find themselves living in poverty, with little hope for advancement. Fitting in with the other students in a mainstream school can be difficult for these children. They may also hesitate to bring friends home after school.

Fitting in with other students isn't as big an issue for students living on the reservation. After all, many have similar problems and backgrounds. But, for those leaving the reservations for college or jobs, adjustment can be difficult. They are leaving their more *insular* environment to become part of something unknown. They may become exposed to things such as drugs or promiscuity that might not have been issues on the reservation.

Chapter 5
Haunted by the Past

S o Tanya, are you feeling better about life now that you've gotten more involved with people?"

Tanya's family were sitting around the dining room table, chowing down on steaming plates of take-out Chinese food—Tanya, her mom, and Grandpa Peshlaki.

"I'm not sure, Gramps."

He set down his chopsticks and waited, obviously expecting more of an answer.

Tanya chewed her moo shoo pork slowly. "I can certainly say life is more interesting," she said at last. "I've learned a lot about the rest of the world from Nura. She's experienced things I never dreamed of. And I've been talking more with that gangsta girl . . . I mean Angela. She hangs around the streets near Krystie's place and the library. I still don't do things with the kids at school, though. Somehow, it seems harder to make normal friends than. . ." She searched for words. "Than it does to make friends with needy people."

Grandpa Peshlaki smiled. "Do you feel your life is more in harmony now?"

Tanya shrugged. "I'm not sure. Sometimes, it feels like *hozho*, like I'm walking the beauty way, but in some really bizarre way, not like back on the Rez. But other times I feel like I'm standing on a track between two trains about to crash."

"Wa-wa-warning. This pro . . . product can be dangerous for your el-ha-health." Nura looked up from the label she was reading and smiled. Tanya returned her grin.

"That's great, Nura. Your reading has really improved. Now, what would you do if someone had swallowed that?"

"Call 9-1-1."

"What would you do if they ask you what the person took?"

"Read off the label."

"Can you do that, now?"

Nura did so, stumbling some but pronouncing most of the difficult words on the label correctly.

"And if they ask for your address?"

"My address is 3946 Crenshaw, just south of the Crenshaw and Alameda intersection, Apartment number 34."

"That's great, Nura. I hope you never have to deal with an emergency, but if so—it's important to be prepared."

"Thanks, Tanya." Nura smiled. "You're a big help."

"That's what friends are for, Nura. You got any plans for the weekend?"

"Plans for the weekend?"

"Yeah, you know. See a movie, crash a party, go out with some cute boy?" Tanya giggled.

"Allah be praised—*no!*" Nura shuddered. "Movies . . . parties, they have bad things . . . sex, beer, drugs . . . not right with Holy Koran."

Tanya nodded thoughtfully. "I appreciate the way you live out your faith, Nura. It's good that your family stays true to their traditions."

"And," Nura added, "Father, he will be very, very anger if he ever catch me alone with a boy."

"It's gonna be a while before you can date, huh?"

"My parents will choose the man I marry."

"Really?"

"Yes."

"Wow."

The two girls were silent for a moment, but it was a comfortable silence now. "What about you, Tanya?" Nura asked after a moment. "You . . . how you say that? You have any plans for the weekend?"

Tanya smiled. "Krystie's coming down Saturday, and we'll hang out on the beach. Hey, you're welcome to join us."

"Thank you, Tanya, invitation is very kind of you. I think . . . people on the beach here are very immodest, my father say."

"Well, you're always welcome to hang out with us."

Nura gathered her books into a backpack, Tanya picked up her purse, and the two girls headed out the door.

"You taking the bus home?"

"Yes, route 15."

"I'm going to catch the next bus after that—I'll wait with you."

As they headed out of the library, Tanya spied a familiar figure, clad in baggy black pants and a white sleeveless top.

"Hey, homegirl," Angela called.

"*Hola, amiga,*" replied Tanya, trying to practice her few words of Spanish. She turned to Nura. "I'd like you to meet someone."

Nura was looking nervous; she apparently understood gang attire.

Over the past weeks, Tanya had spent more time with the Guatemalan girl and was beginning to feel more at ease around her. Angela could live up to her name—La Loca— sometimes displaying a frightening lack of common sense. Yet there were other times when she and Tanya clicked.

One day, Angela had asked Tanya to come and meet her aunt Concha. When they arrived at the aunt's house, she was deftly moving dyed wool through a set of upright cords, weaving. Tanya was fascinated, since when she was alive, Grandma Peshlaki had done very similar weaving on a primitive loom in their hogan. When Tanya told Angela, the other girl was also intrigued to see the similarities in culture between their people.

Now Tanya was about to steer Nura toward Angela when a sound like firecrackers diverted her attention. *Kapow!*

Kapow! Time suddenly dissolved into slow motion.

On Tanya's left a dark SUV came down the road, with the passenger side window open and an arm sticking out, holding a handgun, blowing windows apart as the car cruised along slowly.

Next, Tanya watched in horror as Angela reached into her baggy pants and produced an enormous, nickel-plated revolver.

Tanya found herself thinking, *How did she ever fit that cannon into her drawers?*

Angela braced her legs and grasped the gun in both hands, like a cop on a television show. One eye closed, Angela coolly leveled the gun and sighted down the long barrel. It was horrifying, Tanya thought, that Angela could appear so calm, so methodical, as if this lethal exchange were some mundane event.

"No! Angela, no!" Tanya screamed.

Angela turned her head, paused.

The SUV drew closer.

Kapow!

Crash. The library window shattered.

Tanya felt her legs turn weak and then collapse.

And then, a siren wailed from the other end of the street. A black-and-white squad car careened into view. The green SUV spun around, tires smoking, and flew back the way it had come. Angela disappeared, unbelievably quickly, into the bushes.

And only then did Tanya notice Nura.

The Afghan girl had curled into a ball, her hands crossed atop her scarf-covered head, moaning softly.

"Nura?" Tanya picked herself up and knelt on the sidewalk. She put an arm around the other girl's shoulder. "Nura, are you all right?"

There was no answer. Nura seemed unaware of Tanya's presence.

"Nura, are you hurt?" Tanya looked up and down her friend's body: she appeared to be physically unharmed.

"Tanya, Nura—are you girls okay?" The volunteer coordinator, Gloria Gonzalez, came running out from the library, alarm in her eyes.

"I think we're okay, Ms. Gonzalez, but Nura's acting real strange. Like she can't even hear me."

Gloria knelt beside her. "Nura, Nura, can you hear me?"

The girl remained curled in a ball, moaning softly.

"You stay with her, I'll call her parents." Ms. Gonzalez ran back into the library.

Twenty minutes later, a beat-up Honda pulled into the parking lot and a small, weary-looking man stepped out, dressed in a slightly out-of-style suit coat, wrinkled pants, and a checkered *kefiya*. He walked over to his daughter and gently caressed her arm, speaking quietly in words Tanya could not understand. Nura slowly uncurled, then pushed herself up on one arm, but her eyes still seemed unfocused.

Then for the first time, the gentleman seemed to notice Tanya. "You Tanya?"

"Yes."

"Thank you . . . for teach Nura, and be friend."

Tanya had trouble finding the right words, so she nodded and said nothing.

"In our country . . . bad things." The man was obviously searching for the right words as well. "Nura . . . hurt inside, in her feelings."

Tanya found her voice. "I'm very sorry. Will she be okay?"

"She okay. We go home."

Her father took Nura by the arm, and the two headed for their car, just as Ms. Gonzalez joined them. As Nura's father drove her out of the lot, Gloria turned to Tanya.

"You must be pretty freaked out."

"Yeah, I guess you could say that."

"Many immigrants from war-torn countries suffer from PTSD, you know."

"From what?"

"Post-traumatic stress disorder. When they see acts of violence, or feel threatened, it sends them back to the traumas they suffered in the past."

"Oh."

"Yes. I hope her father will see a psychologist, but some traditional Afghans are skeptical of Western mental health services. And speaking of traumatic experiences, are you up for the bus ride home after this? I could give you a ride."

"Thanks, Ms. Gonzalez, but my friend Krystie lives pretty close, I think I'll walk over to her house."

"Well, God bless you, *querida*. I hope you have a peaceful evening after all this."

"Thanks. I hope so too."

As Tanya headed down the sidewalk, she wrestled with her thoughts. How could she help someone like Angela, so steeped in violence? And how could she be any help to Nura, who apparently had emotional problems on top of the challenges the Afghan girl faced adjusting to American culture? How could Tanya possibly walk in beauty in such a broken world?

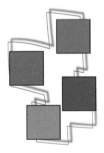

Other Issues for the Immigrant Child

Although problems with language and stereotypes are probably the most significant and most prevalent in this population, children's mental health is also a concern for many. It should be remembered that before coming to the United States or Canada, many of these children were victims of or witnesses to acts of extreme cruelty and violence, experiences so horrendous so as to tax our imaginations. Many know nothing but war. In addition to problems that come with moving to a new country whose language

Children growing up in Afghanistan—like this young girl—face danger and violence that most North American children have never experienced. When these children come to North America, it is often difficult for them to leave behind their fears and sorrows.

and customs they do not know, children who have experienced such traumas can suffer psychologically from such issues as trust, security, and forming relationships.

Helping Immigrants and True Native Populations Adjust

Yes, it can be difficult for immigrant children (and children of immigrants) and those of Native populations to fit in with classmates and the mainstream world. But, all is not lost. There are programs available to aid in achieving success.

Schools have come to realize that they will face increasing numbers of students for whom English is not their first language. Depending on the immigration demographics of their particular areas, some schools have classes taught in Spanish, Vietnamese, or Mandarin Chinese, among other languages. A study by the University of Michigan found there were three primary bilingual methods used to teach students. The *transitional* method is when literacy is taught entirely in the student's native language for a few years; slowly the lessons are changed until they eventually all become taught in English. With a *paired* program, the student is taught in English and her native language at different times of the school day. The third method, *two-way*, teaches the subject in both the native language and English.

Some schools use *English immersion* to teach immigrant children and others less proficient in English. Many believe this to be the quickest way to learn English, as students spend most of the day in regular classrooms where they are taught almost exclusively in English.

Remedial classes and other forms of additional academic help may also be available for the immigrant student. Unfortunately, reduced school budgets have seen such programs scaled back or eliminated in some districts. In certain cases, organizations like the Boys and Girls Clubs have been able to step in and provide assistance for students in need. In addition to academic assistance, such groups also provide

The flood of immigrants moving into the United States from Mexico is a source of ongoing political controversy. While the politicians battle, the children of these immigrants face many challenges.

socialization opportunities—and chances simply to have fun—to the children.

Many communities, especially larger ones, have organizations whose purpose is to help immigrants adjust to their new homes. Some provide or can recommend sources for obtaining financial assistance, housing, medical care, and counseling. They also provide a place to enjoy being with other immigrants facing the same difficulties.

Government- and faith-based support systems are also available in almost all locations. Though government funding for some support services has been cut—in some cases drastically—faith-based services have become more active and visible in the immigrant community. In many cases, assistance is given regardless of immigrant status.

The United States and Canada were founded through immigration. For many years, it was said that America was a melting pot. People came to North America and assimilated into an "American." Today, that's different. People come to America, and, while trying to fit in, they do so *and* maintain their differences. We're more like a salad—or perhaps a taco—with the individual ingredients still visible.

Another Way of Being Different: Religion

It is pretty easy to understand how someone's quality of life can be affected by such factors as being poor or being an immigrant. But, there are other ways that people can be culturally deprived.

Since most of the people in the United States and Canada are religious, it might be difficult to see how religion can make a person culturally different. In most cases, it doesn't. But, in other cases it can.

Islam, for instance, is the world's fastest-growing religion. The word is derived from the Arabic word salam, which is often interpreted as meaning "peace," or "submission." A Muslim is a follower of Islam, a person who submits to the will of God.

Most religious historians view Islam as having been founded in 622 CE by Muhammad the Prophet who lived from about 570 to 632. The religion started in Mecca, when the angel Jibril read the first revelation to Muhammad. Islam is the youngest of the world's main religions: Christianity, Islam, Hinduism, and Buddhism. However, many if not most of the followers

A young Muslim practices his faith. Daily prayer is a fundamental part of Islam.

of Islam believe that Islam existed before Muhammad was born. From this perspective, Islam's origins date back to the creation of the world, and Muhammad was the last and the greatest of a series of Prophets that includes Abraham, Moses, and Jesus.

The Koran (also spelled the Qur'an) is considered by Muslims to be the literal, undistorted word of God, and is the central religious text of Islam. Muslims believe that the Koran was revealed to the prophet Muhammad by God through the Angel Gabriel on numerous occasions between the years 610 and up until Muhammad's death in 632. In addition to memorizing his revelations, his followers had written them down on parchments, stones, and leaves, to preserve the revelation.

The Shahadah is the Islamic **creed**. In Arabic, the word means "to testify" or "to bear witness." When Muslims recite the Shahadah—"There is no god but Allah, and Muhammad is the messenger of Allah"— they are affirming their belief in God's oneness and Muhammad's authority as God's messenger.

Prayer is a vital piece of Muslims' faith. Five times a day, they are required to offer up prayers to Allah. Muslims who live close to a mosque may be called to prayer by a loudspeaker from the mosque, but those who do not, use the position of the sun to tell them when to pray.

Zakat—charity—is yet another vital aspect of Islam. The Arab word means "to grow in goodness" or "to increase in purity." It requires Muslims to spend a fixed portion of their income on the poor and needy; on those whose "hearts need to be reconciled"; and on slaves, those in debt, and travelers.

The Islamic faith shares many common elements with both Christianity and Judaism—but many people in today's post-9/11 world have come to equate Islam with terrorism. A recent Gallup poll found that 39 percent of respondents felt at least some prejudice against Muslims. Thirty-nine percent also favored requiring Muslims—including American citizens—to carry special IDs "as a means of preventing terrorist attacks in the United States." The poll also found that about one-third of the respondents believed that all American Muslims were sympathetic to the terrorist group al-Qaeda. Only 22 percent would be willing to have Muslims as neighbors.

When 75 percent of the people in the United States and Canada are Christians, worshipping God in a different way may put a person at a cultural disadvantage. She may not understand vocabulary, values, and assumptions that the average North American takes for granted. But when that person also has to face prejudice and even hatred, her life is even more complicated and difficult.

Perhaps Not So Different After All

Hear O Israel, the Lord our God, the Lord is One Blessed be the Name of His glorious kingdom for ever and ever.

Those are the opening words to the Shema, one of the most famous of all Jewish prayers. Like Islam's Shahadah, the Shema is a profession of faith, a pledge to follow God. The prayer is recited when getting up in the morning and before going to bed at night. The Shema is the first prayer taught to a Jewish child, and it is the last words a Jew says before death.

Charity is also an integral part of Judaism. Tzedakah is Hebrew for charity. Just like the English concept of charitable acts, tzedakah means giving aid to the poor and needy, and to worthy causes. However, the idea behind tzedakah is a bit different. One usually associates the word charity with kindness and generosity, especially by someone who is wealthy toward someone who is not. The word tzedakah comes from the Hebrew root tzade-dalet-qof, which means justice or fairness. As in Islam's practice of zakat, the Jewish act of tzedakah is a duty, which must be done even by those in need. Under Jewish law, individuals must give one-tenth of their income to the poor. Individuals living in or near poverty are allowed to donate less.

Tzedakah's importance in the Jewish faith cannot be understated. It is one of three things that can bring forgiveness of sins. The others are repentance and prayer.

Chapter 6
Blood on the Street

Where do I draw the line with a friend who's in a gang? Tanya stared out the bus window into the dark streets of Los Angeles. She didn't know the answer to the question.

She had been avoiding Angela for several weeks after the incident outside the library. While she and the Guatemalan girl shared the experience of both being Natives in the big city, Tanya realized they were worlds apart in other ways. Sometimes Angela seemed capable of responsible decisions, yet Tanya knew she was involved with really bad stuff. Tanya was especially concerned that Angela's baby would be due soon, making it even more important that the soon-to-be mother turn her life around. Yet as long as Angela remained "La Loca," Tanya doubted they could be friends.

But an hour ago, Angela had phoned her. She had an expensive cell phone, but Tanya had never had courage to ask how she got it.

"I'm jumping out of 13th Street Gang," Angela's voice said softly in Tanya's ear. "I'm lowering my flag."

"But I thought the Florencias would get you, if you did that."

"They might. But they'll probably get me if I stay, too."

Tanya was silent; she didn't know what to say. "I'm proud of you, Angela," she said finally.

"Thanks Tanya, but . . . I'm scared—terrified. Could you meet me at Tía Concha's apartment? I just need to talk to someone who's not in La Vida Loca."

"Yeah, I'll get on the bus. See ya soon, G-girl—ah, ex-G-girl."

Then everything went wrong. First, Tanya missed the bus from Main Street in Huntington Beach, next the Crenshaw connecting bus was so full of people that it whizzed right by her. Tanya kept trying to call Angela back, but she wouldn't answer.

Tanya felt like a dark wind was blowing its chill way into her soul. Something wasn't right about this evening.

As the bus pulled up at the stop in front of the library, where Tanya would get off and walk three blocks to Tía Concha's apartment, Tanya noticed an odd blue and red flicker illumining a side street. As soon as she stepped off the bus, she felt drawn toward the eerie scene.

Three police cars, pale as ghosts in the flickering light, were parked in the alley. A small crowd stood on the side of the street, young and old, some wearing their gang colors. The scene was focused on a crumpled figure, lying in a dark red pool in the middle of the street.

As she walked slowly closer, Tanya tried not to face what she was seeing.

Baggy pants.

White tube top.

Bulging abdomen.

"*No!*"

Tanya sank to her knees on the sidewalk, and then she turned away and vomited into the gutter. The crowd near her murmured—but Tanya didn't care.

How could they look?

How could they look and not retch at the sight?

Now she became aware of a wailing voice beside her. A small woman, dressed in a faded skirt and cheap-looking sweater, knelt on the ground, crying out and sobbing. After a few minutes, the woman composed herself, dabbed her eyes with her sweater, and turned to look at Tanya.

Tanya recognized the high cheekbones, thick hair, and the same look that had been in Angela's eyes. The woman was breathing in short, stricken gasps.

"You're her mom?" Tanya whispered.

"*Sí. Eres Tanya?*"

The Navajo girl nodded.

"*Fueras su amiga mejor.*"

"I was . . . her best friend?"

"*Sí.*" The woman spoke through her tears. "*Gracias.*"

Angela's mother turned back to her daughter's body and brushed a hair off Angela's still face.

Behind her, Tanya heard angry voices. "Effin' Florencias. This is our turf. They can't do this. We're gonna smoke 'em."

"I got my nine, let's ride."

"First ones we see—bam!"

"Blow 'em straight to *el diablo.*"

Something inside of Tanya –maybe it was her grief, or maybe her anger—gave her a courage she had never known or even imagined she could feel. She stood, turned, and faced a half dozen people her age, all dressed in baggy pants, white shirts, and the familiar kerchief tied on their pant legs. "I can't believe all you're thinking of is revenge!"

They glared at her, their eyes flat and dark. "You *loca?* Know who we are?"

Tanya nodded. "I was her friend, too. And I know how she got into your gang—when Lupita died, and she went on a ride like you're going on now. I'm tellin' you, it won't stop tonight. You'll kill, then they'll kill, and on and on. Death after death. How many more have to die in 13th Street and Florencia? How many more Angelas? If she was really your home girl, you'd honor her by ending the killing—now."

Tanya turned and walked back toward the bus stop, hearing their angry cursing fade away behind her. She sat down inside the Plexiglas enclosure, put her head in her hands, and sobbed. Mostly her tears were for the loss of a friend, but there was something besides that, she realized.

Fear.

Having faced up to the gang members, all her bravado now faded, and she began to shake. What if the buses had run on time? If they had, *she* would have been standing beside Angela when it happened. In her mind's eye, Tanya could clearly see two bodies bleeding onto the street.

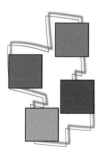

Violence and Cultural Differences

Violence has taken place between cultural groups in North America since the eighteenth century, when settlers from different nations first came to the continent. During the early to mid-nineteenth centuries, violent rioting occurred between Protestant "Nativists" and recently arriving Irish-Catholic immigrants, reaching its height during the 1840s and 1850s in North American cities. Chinese immigrants were the next group to face racial prejudice, particularly in the West (both in the United States and Canada), and tensions between North Americans and Italian immigrants caused unrest during the late nineteenth century and on into the early twentieth.

In many cases, to protect themselves (physically, emotionally, and socially), immigrants formed close-knit groups. In some cases these groups turned into gangs.

What Is a Gang?

A gang is a group of teens and young adults who hang out together and are involved in joint violent, illegal, or criminal activity. They generally give themselves a common name or symbol, and they often wear a certain type of clothing or display some other identifying item. Young adults may turn to gangs in their search for identity and belonging.

Gang activity in the United States has risen sharply since the 1970s, when gangs were active in less than half the states—compared to now, when every state reports youth gang activity. Although once thought to

Gangs offer young adults a sense of belonging, a source of identity, and an answer to the loneliness and angst of being an adolescent. Unfortunately, gangs are also usually violent, destructive, and criminal.

be an inner-city problem, gang violence has spread to many rural and small-town communities throughout North America. At last count, there were more than 24,500 different youth gangs around the United States, and more than 772,500 teens and young adults were members of gangs. Youth gangs are responsible for much of the serious violence in the United States. In schools and neighborhoods where they are active, they create a climate of fear and increase the amount of violence and criminal behavior.

Although some gang members are as young as twelve, the average age is between seventeen and eighteen. However, as many as half of youth gang members are eighteen or older. These older members are much more likely to be involved in serious and violent crimes than are younger members. Fortunately,

FAST FACT

Teens that are gang members are much more likely than other teens to commit serious and violent crimes. For example, a survey in Denver found that while only 14 percent of teens were gang members, they were responsible for committing 89 percent of the serious violent crimes.

for most teens, gang membership is a brief phase: one-half to two-thirds of teen gang members leave the gang by the end of their first year.

Male teens are much more likely to join gangs than female teens. Police reports indicate that only about 6 percent of gang members are female and that only about a third of gangs have any female members. Female gang members are less likely to be involved in criminal behavior than males, but that doesn't mean they're not dangerous: 78 percent of female gang members reported being involved in gang fights, 65 percent reported carrying a weapon for protection, and 39 percent reported attacking someone with a weapon.

Chapter 7
Ancient Ways

I need help, Grandpa. I'm going crazy. I keep seeing Angela on the street, bloody and crumpled. It's like she haunts me. Can you perform a healing ceremony?"

It was a week after Angela's murder: Tanya sat on the couch, opposite her mother and grandfather. Grandpa Peshlaki nodded gravely.

"You came close to the death of your friend, and her *chindi*—her departing spirit— infected your soul. We must sing a Night Chant for you—and it must be done in a hogan, within the sacred lands."

"We have to go back to the Rez then?"

"Yes. We should leave first thing tomorrow and—"

"What?" Tanya's mom interrupted. "Your big gallery presentation at the museum is on Thursday. You can't go now."

"I'll just tell them a family crisis came up. They will understand."

"No, Papa, they won't understand. This is a big deal. Don't you care about your art career?"

"My art is a gift from the Holy Ones—and they know my granddaughter's life is more important than hanging around a bunch of people drinking wine and talking about my paintings."

"But, Papa," Tanya's mom insisted, "it's not some life-threatening illness. Can't this wait?"

Grandpa Peshlaki gave his daughter a stern stare. "We leave tomorrow, at sunrise."

"Thank you, Grandpa." Tanya thought she had never loved the old man more than at this moment.

A single large fire illumined the interior of the hogan, casting flickering shadows from the dozen or so people seated around the interior of the dwelling. The smell of mesquite smoke was practically intoxicating in the enclosure, and Grandpa Peshlaki's singing, accompanied by the rhythmic rattle of ceremonial gourds, created even more of a hypnotic effect. For three nights, the singing had gone on. Tanya couldn't understand all the ancient words, but the healing cadence of the chants soothed her heart. She stared into the fire, letting the sounds sink into her soul, for hours on end.

Around midnight, she noticed the flames changing: they weren't just random patterns anymore but images. The flickering lights seemed to be drawing her out of the mundane world, into an entirely different location. Now Tanya perceived herself to be standing below a hilly ridge that was silhouetted against a reddish sky. If this inexplicable change of scene happened under any other circumstances she would be scared out of her wits. But this was a sacred ceremony, and the ordinary earth and supernatural realm were not so far away in such a setting. This must be the world of the spirit people, she realized.

Atop the ridge, she saw dancers; the Yeis—supernatural beings. They leaped and turned in synchronized motions, as if all of these Holy Ones had one heart and mind. In the midst of the Holy Ones, Tanya saw a girl, oddly dressed. In her vision-state, Tanya rushed up the hillside to gain a closer look; her feet flew effortlessly up the rocky side of the ridge, as though her body were weightless, for everything is different in the place of the Holy Ones.

Now Tanya could see the girl clearly: she was dressed in a handmade dress and matching head scarf, covered with colorful woven designs. In her arms, the girl carried a tiny bundle—a newborn baby. As the dancers turned, Tanya could see the girl's face—it was Angela! Tanya caught her breath. *"She is no longer La Loca,"* she thought, *"This is her true self—Angela of the Jaguar Clan—freed to dance with the Holy Ones."* The spirit girl looked up, saw Tanya, and their eyes connected. Angela flashed a smile, waved at her earth-bound friend, then skipped away over the crest of the hill with the dancing spirits.

The flame images dissolved; now they were just random jets of burning mesquite. The chanting continued on for hours.

Finally, as the light of morning crept through the smoke hole atop the hogan, Grandpa Peshlaki's husky voice slowed, quieted, stopped. The only sound within the earthen structure was the crackling of the fire. Then, the singer spoke to his granddaughter. "The *chindi* has gone from you tonight."

He said it with the same matter-of-fact tone one might use to describe the changing weather.

Tanya nodded in agreement.

"You are restored to *hozho* then. Your life is once more in sacred balance."

Tanya let out a long breath of relief and joy. She knew her grandfather was right. "Thank you," she whispered.

"But your testing is not over, granddaughter. You must return to the big city. You must learn to walk in peace even in the midst of a disordered world."

Tanya felt her heart sink.

Grandpa Peshlaki continued, in a still small voice, as if they were the only two people in the holy enclosure.

"Tanya, do you remember your real name, the Navajo name you were given at birth?"

She did, though she never dared to utter the name aloud, as her Navajo name was sacred; anyone learning her true name could use its power against her. But she could speak her secret name in this sacred space.

"Say your name."

"Warrior Girl."

Grandpa Peshlaki nodded; "That is your true name—your name-of-power. It is a strong name, because the Holy Ones knew you would face many challenges."

There was a lengthy pause, intended to add gravity to the *haatali's* concluding words.

"As you re-enter the city with many peoples and many tests, remember—you are Warrior Girl. Go in the strength of your true name."

"Are you planning to leave for the Rez right after graduation?" Krystie asked several weeks later.

Tanya and Krystie were sitting on the couch in Krystie's apartment, munching on chips and watching VH1.

"I don't know."

Krystie raised an eyebrow; "You might stay in California?"

"I don't want to be hasty. It's an important decision."

"Well, I'd sure love it if you stayed. There are millions of people in LA—but it wouldn't be the same without you."

"I'd miss you too, Krystie, and that's one big reason I might stay here. And besides. . ." Tanya paused for a moment to choose her words. "Before now, I wanted to go back to the Rez for the wrong reasons. I was afraid of this city, wanting to run away in fear. If I do go back to the Rez, I'll be going *to* something—because of the good things I can do on Navajo Nation—but I won't leave this city defeated."

"Wow! That's great."

Tanya smiled; she seemed to be doing more of that lately. "I've gotta run. Have to meet Nura at the library in five minutes."

"How's the tutoring going?"

"Good. She's learning a lot, and she's warming up to life in the city."

"I'd say you're warming up, too."

As soon as Tanya walked through the big glass doors and metal detectors at the library, coordinator Gloria Gonzales rushed up to meet her.

"Tanya, I've been waiting for you."

"Is something wrong, Ms. Gonzales?"

"Oh, no! But I have a surprise. Come—*ándele*." She took Tanya's arm and led her to a room used for conferences in the back of the library.

Nura stood there with an enormous smile, accompanied by her father and three others whom Tanya assumed were Nura's mother and sisters. At once, the entire group surrounded Tanya, hugging her and talking quickly in the language of their homeland.

"Nura, what's this all about—what's happening?"

Nura held up a medicine bottle. "It's about this!"

Tanya was still confused. "What. . . ?"

Nura explained, "Remember that lesson you teach me about medicine?"

"Uh . . . I'm not sure I do."

"The lesson was what to do in emergency."

"Oh, yes."

"Two days ago, sister Ilana, she was sick. Father went to doctor, then to store for medicine."

Tanya nodded, still puzzled.

Nura's father joined in. "The store, make wrong medicine—very bad. When Ilana take medicine, she get terrible sick . . . almost like die."

Tanya's eyes widened, imagining the scene.

Nura's father continued, "Nura, she run to phone . . . tell them what you taught her. Hospital people come quick . . . say Nura's call saved Ilana's life."

"All because of what you teach me!" Nura threw her arms around Tanya's neck.

The next morning, a Saturday, Tanya's mom stopped outside the door of her daughter's room and asked, "Tanya—do you want to go to the free concert at the beach with me this afternoon?"

Tanya shook her head. "Thanks, Mom, but I'm going shopping."

"With Krystie?"

"No, I'm going with Vanna."

"With who?"

"The Asian girl at school. She's always asking if I want to hang out with her."

Tanya's mother's eyebrows went up. "I thought you didn't trust her."

"I don't know if I do or not, but I'll find out soon."

"What made you decide to go shopping with her?"

"Just thought I'd try and make some new friends."

A funny-sounding car horn beeped from the street in front of their condo. Tanya went and opened the door.

A decrepit van idled in the street, and Vanna—dressed perfectly as always—stepped out of the vehicle's side door.

Tanya ran to join her. "Hey, Vanna."

"Hey, Tanya. Hope you don't mind, but this shopping trip sort of became a group thing. My Lexus is in the shop from a fender bender, and my friends Josh and Ashley offered to drive us over to Westside Store Parade."

"Yeah, sure that's cool." Then Tanya lowered her voice and asked, "Is that old car safe?"

"Oh, yeah. Josh's surf bus is famous all over town. Looks like he pulled it from a junkyard, but wait till you hear the sound—this old van rocks!"

Tanya noticed her mom standing in the door. "Bye, Mom!" she shouted and waved. The door shut.

Vanna opened the van's side door, and Tanya stepped in. A tall boy with long blond hair turned around in the driver's seat and stuck out his hand. "Hi, I'm Josh."

Next to him, a brunette girl in the front passenger seat chimed in, "And I'm Ashley."

"Nice to meet you" Tanya replied.

She settled into the back bench seat next to Vanna and clipped her seat belt as the van chugged away from the curb, headed for Coast Highway.

This is going to be a whole new adventure, Tanya told herself.

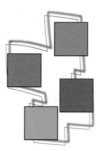

Each of us is unique; we are all "different" in some way. Maybe we look a little different, maybe we speak differently, maybe we believe differently. Because we each have individual gifts and strengths to offer, our differences are what make human society strong.

At the same time, however, human beings are often threatened by differences. They fear that the person who "looks funny" or "acts funny" will hurt them in some way. The injury they fear ranges from concern that these "strangers" will take away jobs and limited resources—to the fear of violence. Unfortunately, fear and distrust tend to breed violence, and it becomes a vicious cycle. According to Tolerance.org, a project of the Southern Poverty Law Center, every hour, somewhere in America, someone

Tolerance and love are the weapons that fight the violence of hate and prejudice.

commits a hate crime; every day, at least eight blacks, three whites, three gays, three Jews, and one Latino become hate crime victims.

Tolerance.org has this to say about these tragic facts as they relate to people who are culturally different:

> Hate in America is a dreadful, daily constant. The dragging death of a black man in Jasper, Texas; the crucifixion of a gay man in Laramie, Wyo.; and post-9/11 hate crimes against hundreds of Arab Americans, Muslim Americans and Sikhs are not "isolated incidents." They are eruptions of a nation's intolerance.
>
> Bias is a human condition, and American history is rife with prejudice against groups and individuals because of their race, religion, disability, sexual orientation, or other differences. The 20th century saw major progress in outlawing discrimination, and most Americans today support integrated schools and neighborhoods. But stereotypes and unequal treatment persist, an atmosphere often exploited by hate groups.
>
> When bias motivates an unlawful act, it is considered a hate crime. Race and religion inspire most hate crimes, but hate today wears many faces. Bias incidents (eruptions of hate where no crime is committed) also tear communities apart—and threaten to escalate into actual crimes.
>
> According to FBI statistics, the greatest growth in hate crimes in recent years is against Asian

Americans and the gay and lesbian community. Once considered a Southern phenomenon, today most hate crimes are reported in the North and West.

And these numbers are just the tip of the iceberg. Law enforcement officials acknowledge that hate crimes—similar to rape and family violence crimes—go under-reported, with many victims reluctant to go to the police, and some police agencies not fully trained in recognizing or investigating hate crimes.

Tolerance is the only way to break the cycle of hatred and violence. When we learn to accept those who are different, we can begin to build a better, more peaceful world. As Tolerance.org affirms:

Our experience shows that one person, acting from conscience and love, is able to neutralize bigotry. Imagine, then, what an entire community, working together, might do.

Glossary

Aboriginal: A member of any of the peoples who inhabited Canada before the arrival of European settlers.

assimilation: The process in which one group takes on the cultural and other traits of a larger group with the purpose of fitting in.

circumventing: Finding a way of avoiding restrictions imposed by a rule or law without actually breaking it.

consensus: General or widespread agreement among all the members of a group.

contemporaries: Individuals who are the same age.

contiguous: Sharing a boundary or physically touching each other.

creed: A set of religious beliefs.

empathize: To understand the feelings and thoughts of another.

enclaves: Distinct groups that live or operate together within a larger community.

ethnicity: Ethnic affiliation.

foreclosure: The legal process by which property is taken away from someone with a mortgage because of a failure to make payments.

gross income: Income earned before deductions such as tax and other expenses have been made.

industrialized: A country or group adapted to the industrial methods of production and manufacturing.

initiative: A plan, strategy, or effort designed to deal with a particular problem.

insular: Physically or emotionally removed from others.

mandated reporters: Individuals such as child-care providers, teachers, health-care workers, and police officers who are required by law to report suspected cases of child abuse to appropriate social services agencies.

median: The middle value.

net incomes: Income that remains after deductions such as tax and other expenses have been made.

ostracized: Banished or excluded from society or from a group.

permanent resident: A non-citizen who has fulfilled requirements allowing him to reside within a country despite not being a citizen, and is allowed to travel outside of the country.

profound: Strong, intense.

relative: Considered in comparison with something else.

second-generation immigrants: Native-born children of immigrants.

sporadic: Occurring occasionally at intervals that have no apparent pattern.

visas: Official endorsements in a passport authorizing the bearer to enter or leave, and travel in or through a particular country or region.

World Bank: A specialized agency of the United Nations that authorizes loans to member nations for the purpose of reconstruction and development; its official name is the International Bank for Reconstruction and Development.

Further Reading

Balkin, Karen F., and James D. Torr. *Current Controversies—Civil Rights*. Farmington Hills, Mich.: Greenhaven Press, 2004.

Bode, Janet. *The Colors of Freedom: Immigrant Stories*. New York: Franklin Watts, 2000.

Dudley, William, and Louise I. Gerdes (eds.). *Gangs*. Farmington Hills, Mich.: Greenhaven Press, 2004.

Gerdes, Louise I. (ed.). *Current Controversies—Immigration*. Farmington Hills, Mich.: Greenhaven Press, 2005.

Hunter, Miranda. *The Story of Latino Civil Rights: Fighting for Justice*. Broomall, Pa.: 2005.

Williams, Mary E. (ed.). *Discrimination*. Farmington Hills, Mich.: Greenhaven Press, 2002.

Worth, Richard, Leslie Berger, and Austin Sarat. *Gangs and Crime*. New York: Chelsea House, 2001.

For More Information

Facts for Teens: Youth Violence
www.safeyouth.org

Southern Poverty Law Center
www.splcenter.org

Teen Project RACE
www.projectrace.com/teenprojectrace

TeenInk
teenink.com/Resources/PublishingR.html

Thirteen
www.thirteen.org

The Troubles Teens Face
www.dianedew.com/teens.htm

Publisher's note:
The Web sites listed on this page were active at the time of publication. The publisher
is not responsible for Web sites that have changed their addresses or discontinued
operation since the date of publication. The publisher will review and update the
Web-site list upon each reprint.

Bibliography

"Anti-Islam Prejudice." http://www.islamawareness.net/Islamophobia/eu_report.html.

"A Baseline Definition of Culture." http://www.wsu.edu:8001/vcwsu/commons/topics/culture/culture-definition.html.

Build up Bethlehem, Build up Hope. http://www.cbmin.org.

Canadian Pensioners Concerned. "Poverty in Canada." http://www.canpension.ca/pages/newsstories/poverty.html.

Flippin, Susan Saunders. "Cultural and Linguistic Diversity and the Special Education Workforce: A Critical Overview." *Journal of Special Education*, 2004.

Grieco, Elizabeth M. *Estimates of the Nonimmigrant Population in the United States: 2004*. Washington, D.C.: Department of Homeland Security, Office of Immigration Statistics, 2006.

Islam World. http://www.islamworld.net.

Marcus, Adam. "Boost From Poverty Helps Kids' Mental Health." http://www.hon.ch/News/HSN/515544.html.

Noguera, Pedro A. "Responding to the Crisis Confronting Black Youth: Providing Support Without Furthering Marginalization." *In Motion*. http://www.inmotionmagazine.com/pncc1.html.

Pellino, Karen M. "The Effects of Poverty on Teaching and Learning." http://www.teach-nology.com/tutorials/teaching/poverty/print.htm.

"Program Ideas for Exploring." http://www.learning-for-life.org/exploring/socialservices/ideas.html.

"Social Consequences of Poverty." http://www.mapleleafweb.com/features/general/poverty/consequences.html.

Statistics Canada. http://www40.statcan.ca/101/cst01/demo34a.htm?sdi=immigrant.

Street Gangs Resource Center. http://www.streetgangs.com

Tolerance.org. "10 Ways to Fight Hate." http://www.tolerance.org/10_ways/index.html.

Unitarian Universalist Association. "Youth Welfare." http://www.uua.org/actions/youth/63welfare.html.

Index

Picture Credits

CIA, Jamie Carroll: p. 90
Harding House Publisher Service, Ben Stewart: pp. 29, 74, 76
iStockphoto: pp. 17, 27, 42
       Bratslavsky, Natalia: p. 57
       Collado, Juan: p. 39
       Gearhart, Rosemarie: p. 103
       Honeycutt, M. Eric: p. 34
       Nordmann, Jean: p. 88
       Rodriguez, Daniel: p. 58
       Schmidt, Chris: p. 38
       Schupp, Bonnie: p. 116
       Walsh, William: p. 37
Jupiter Images: pp. 41, 55, 60, 92

Authors

Kenneth McIntosh is a freelance writer living in northern Arizona with his family. He has written two dozen educational books, and taught at junior high, high school, and community college levels.

Ida Walker is a graduate of the University of Northern Iowa in Cedar Falls. She attended graduate school at Syracuse University in Syracuse, New York. She lives and works in Upstate New York.

Series Consultants

Mary Jo Dudley is the director of the Cornell Farmworker Program and a faculty member in Cornell University's Department of Development Sociology. She is bilingual and has numerous years of experience of working with issues related to Latino communities in the U.S., U.S./ Latin American relations, and migration. Her publications include Heroes, Warriors or Gangsters: Understanding the Trauma of Immigration through Narratives, a book chapter based on her research with Latino gangs in California. Her book, Transforming Cultures in the Americas (Cornell University, 2000), explores how various Latin American communities experience the immigration process to the US. She also was the former director of Cornell Program on Gender and Global Change, and the former Associate Director of the Cornell Latin American Studies Program.

Cindy Croft, M.A.Ed., is the Director of the Center for Inclusive Child Care (CICC) at Concordia University, St. Paul, MN. The CICC is a comprehensive resource network for promoting and supporting inclusive early childhood and school-age programs and providers with Project EXCEPTIONAL training and consultation, and other resources at www.inclusivechildcare. org. In addition to working with the CICC, Ms. Croft is faculty at Concordia University and Minneapolis Community and Technical College.